THE CHANGING RAIL SCENE IN SOUTH WALES 1990s–PRESENT

JOHN JACKSON

AMBERLEY

First published 2024

Amberley Publishing
The Hill, Stroud
Gloucestershire, GL5 4EP

www.amberley-books.com

Copyright © John Jackson, 2024

The right of John Jackson to be identified as
the Author of this work has been asserted in
accordance with the Copyrights, Designs and
Patents Act 1988.

ISBN 978 1 3981 2353 3 (print)
ISBN 978 1 3981 2354 0 (ebook)

British Library Cataloguing in Publication Data.
A catalogue record for this book is available from
the British Library.

Typesetting by Hurix Digital, India.
Printed in the UK.

Contents

Introduction

I can vividly recall my first adventure to South Wales over half a century ago. The date was 16 February 1969 to be precise. It is etched in my memory for two reasons. Firstly, it was to be my first experience of a 'shed bash' in the area, including the depots of Cardiff, Newport and Severn Tunnel Junction. Secondly, our minibus trip included a visit to the scrapyard of Dai Woodham, at Barry, which was fast becoming a shrine among enthusiasts due to it being home to over 200 steam locomotives awaiting their cutting fate.

Many of those steam locomotives were to be saved from the cutter's torch for younger generations to enjoy, albeit at preservation lines around the UK. That day in 1969 saw the beginning of my love affair with the railways of South Wales. My trusty notebook from that Sunday also reveals an impressive haul of Class 37 and Class 47 locomotives, as well as nearly forty diesel shunters recorded, in addition to the Barry steam list.

Those two main-line diesel locomotive classes were to be the area's mainstays through to the start of the period under review in this publication. By the start of the 1990s, Class 56 and Class 60 locos were also in evidence. The railways of that era were about to undergo a decade of considerable change, not least because of the impact of the move from a nationalised to a privatised rail network. The ubiquitous Class 66 General Motors locomotive was also to make its first appearance on rail freight traffic towards the end of that decade.

In this book, we take a look at these various classes of diesel locomotives through the 1990s, the decade of rail privatisation, and trace the changes brought about by the now-private freight operators in the thirty years since. Of course, the ubiquitous Class 66 locomotives were to continue to play a major part throughout this period and do so today.

Not surprisingly, the South Wales area's passenger-carrying railway has altered significantly during the same period. The full extent of these changes will become evident in the pages that follow. Various parts of the railway's supporting services had already been sold off during the 1970s and 1980s. These services were as diverse as Sealink (ferries), British Transport Hotels and British Rail Engineering Ltd. The railways were then sold off under the Railways Act 1993. Space precludes the inclusion of a full history of events and ownership since then. Significantly, in 2000 the Wales and Borders franchise was announced and this was to incorporate most passenger services within Wales, with yet more being added in the next two or three years. The result was the appointment of Arriva to operate this franchise for a fifteen-year period commencing in December 2003, trading under the Arriva Trains Wales branding.

When this franchise was due for renewal in 2018, Arriva withdrew from the bidding process and the franchise changed hands with Keolis/Amey Wales appointed for what was expected to be a further fifteen-year contract. The Covid-19 pandemic was to deliver a huge, unexpected blow to rail travel across the UK, and South Wales was no exception. A substantial fall in passenger numbers led to the intervention of the Welsh government in early 2021. Transport for Wales (TfW) was created as a nonprofit business to replace Keolis/Amey on this franchise under its powers as 'Operator as last resort'. This effectively placed the majority of South Wales' passenger services under public ownership. This included the management of approximately 250 stations in the region. The local provider of engineering and maintenance services in the area, Pullman Rail, also came under TfW ownership later in 2021, with its continued operation from Cardiff's Canton depot complex.

Outside of this TfW control, there remain some services in the hands of other passenger operators. Notably, the service linking London Paddington with Cardiff and Swansea had been operated by Great Western Trains from early 1996. Two years later, the company was bought by the First Group and rebranded as First Great Western.

In 1996, Wales and West independently commenced operating other passenger services that connected Cardiff with a number of destinations in the south and west of England, including Brighton, Portsmouth and Penzance. A reorganisation saw those services falling under the 'Wessex Trains' branding in 2001. Yet more re-structuring saw both these London and Wessex services combined under the First Group's ownership as First Greater Western Limited, a company first incorporated in April 2004. Throughout this period the key route between London and Cardiff, but not beyond to Swansea, has seen electrification completed and the iconic diesel High Speed Trains (HSTs) phased out on these services. They have been replaced by bi-mode Intercity Express Trains (IETs) on all GWR's London services. For approaching thirty years, the operator has seen no competition on this core route linking London and South Wales. Under the 'open access' agreement, speculative operator Grand Union Trains Ltd has been given permission to offer alternative services linking the Carmarthen area with London, although the date for commencement of any such service has slipped to 2025 at the very earliest.

The only other passenger operator with regular services to and from Cardiff is CrossCountry Trains. They have provided services from Cardiff to Birmingham, Derby and Nottingham since 2006, when Arriva took over the route from Central Trains. They have operated an almost unchanged hourly service from then until the present day. Although longer distance services using Voyager units no longer serve South Wales, there is a hint of a possible direct service linking Cardiff and Edinburgh to commence in the shorter term.

The traditional South Wales industries have either gone completely or are under serious threat. The South Wales Main Line electrification may have been scaled back with little chance of it reaching Swansea in the foreseeable future. On a more positive note, the conversion of Cardiff city centre for operation of Crossrail continues apace and the Class 398 tram trains will probably be in operation shortly.

Whatever the pros and cons, the scene in South Wales has changed over the last thirty years, but, as this publication hopefully demonstrates, there is still much for anyone with an interest in the area's railways to enjoy.

I trust you enjoy your journey through the pages that follow as much as I have enjoyed compiling them.

John Jackson

Rail Map of South Wales

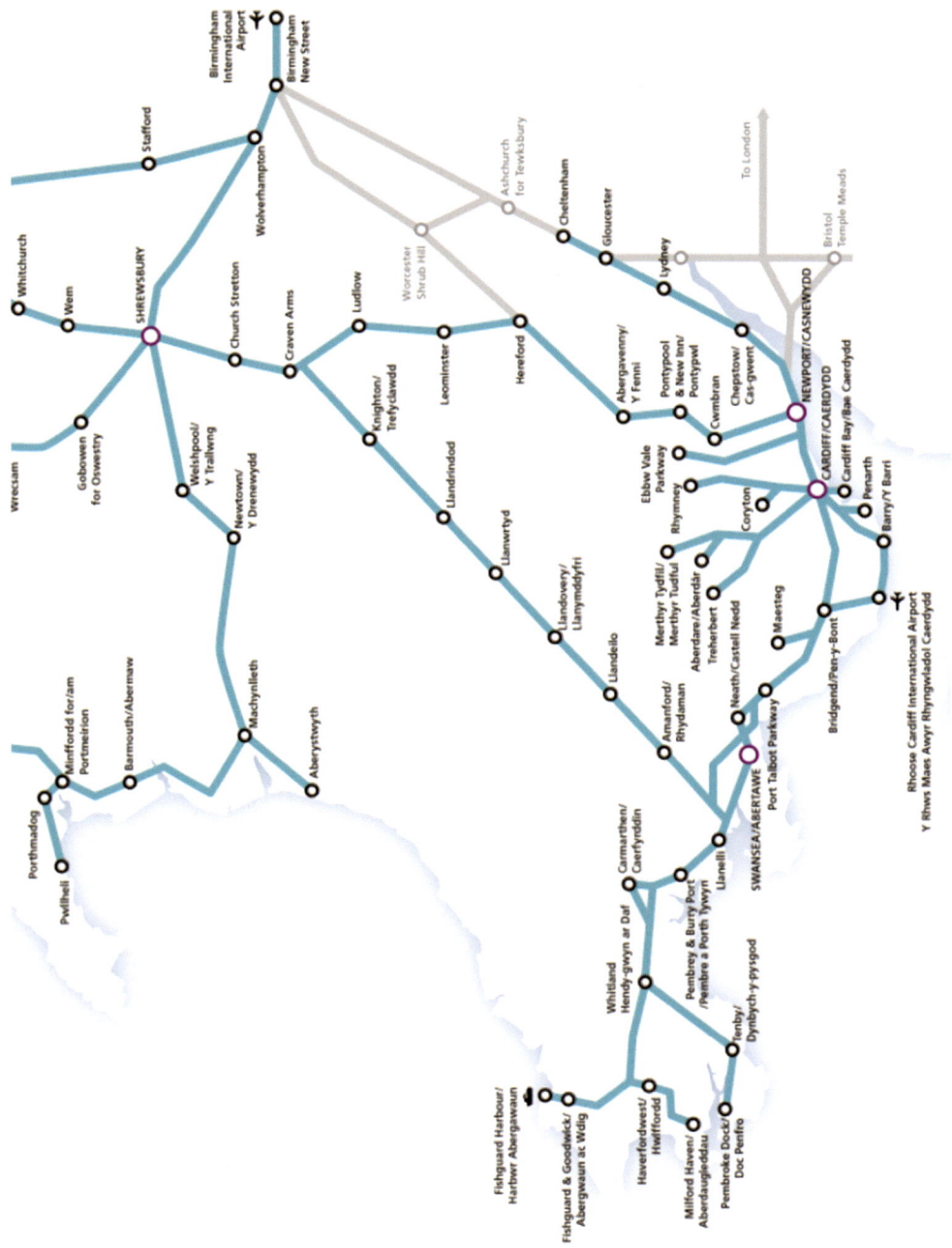

The railway map of South Wales in the twenty-first century. The line to and from Ebbw Vale Parkway has now been extended to Ebbw Vale Town station.

South Wales – Setting the Scene

In the introduction I explained my love affair with South Wales had begun with a trip to the area in 1969, including this view over the rooftops of the steam locos assembled at Dai Woodham's scrapyard at Barry that day.

That scene from Barry has long been consigned to history, along with that day's memory of Severn Tunnel Junction shed, code 86E. The marshalling yard was to close on 12 October 1987. This is the view of the area thirty years later, in 2017.

A revamp of Newport station was unveiled in 2010, to coincide with the area holding golf's Ryder Cup. The Great Western Main Line electrification came to South Wales a decade later.

Cardiff Crossrail have made a major impact on the city centre of the Welsh capital, with building work around Central station seemingly having gone on for many years. This includes the new bus interchange promising better all-round transport connectivity. The Central railway station still acts as a welcoming 'shop window' even in this early morning view in March 2024.

At the beginning of the 1990s, freight services in South Wales were, of course, in the hands of British Rail, with privatisation not yet on the railway horizon. In a typical scene from April 1990, English Electric Type '3' 37294 heads west through Cardiff Central station on a rake of empty tank wagons.

These Type '3' locomotives were to be classified as Class 37s under the 1970s' Total Operations Processing System (TOPS) renumbering scheme and were ever-present on freight services in South Wales in the run-up to rail privatisation in the mid-1990s. In this 1994 view of Newport, 37141 heads light engine through the platform. The town's stabling point at Godfrey Road is seen in the background.

By the 1990s, the days of all locos being painted blue was becoming a thing of the past. In this October 1991 view, 37092 is sporting the livery of the then Civil Engineer's Department. It is seen stabled on Cardiff Canton depot awaiting its next duty.

South Wales was the base for a number of Brush Type '4' locomotives, which were also to be found on the area's freight and mail workings. 47285 was one of these locomotives allocated to Cardiff Canton. It is seen on its home depot in October 1991, in the company of a variety of Class 37 locomotives, as well as a pair of Class 08 diesel shunters. As an avid regular rail enthusiast visitor to the area, I always had an air of anticipation and excitement on crossing the footbridge at the depot entrance as to exactly what would be on view!

As the 1990s began, long-distance passenger services were operated by British Rail under the 'InterCity' branding. This included the regular High Speed Train (HST) services linking South Wales with London's Paddington terminus. HST Power car 43030 has just terminated at Cardiff Central station on a London Paddington arrival in spring 1994.

The first generation of diesel multiple units was to be the mainstay on local passenger services around Cardiff and the Valleys, with some surviving into the 1990s. One of the earliest classes to replace them in South Wales was the Class 143 'Pacer'. Built in the mid-1980s and later transferred from the North East of England, 143612 calls at Newport station in 1994. This unit is working a Regional Railways service to Chepstow.

Non-passenger Traffic in the 1990s

While newspaper traffic on the rail network had ceased in 1988, parcels were still handled by the Rail Express Services (RES) sector during the 1990s. In April 1990, Brush Type '2' loco 31432 waits at Cardiff Central at the head of a short rake of vans.

The shunting of this van traffic necessitated the stabling of a Class 08 diesel shunter in the Cardiff station's platform area. In April 1990, 08932 was being used on this duty. This shunter was to survive for a further fifteen years before being scrapped in 2005.

Further east in South Wales, Newport station also saw regular workings of diesel shunters on local trip workings between the various yards in the Newport area, with 09203 one of the regular performers. On 18 April 1994, 09203 heads eastwards with a mixed rake of wagons.

A couple of weeks later, on 29 April 1994, the same shunter takes a short rake in the opposite direction as it passes through Newport station platform.

In the 1990s, a wide variety of Class 37 English Electric Type '3' locomotives in various liveries and on various duties were operated. This included frequent light-engine moves along the South Wales Main Line, particularly through both Cardiff and Newport stations. In April 1994, 37158 and 37258 wait in Cardiff Central's centre road.

With 37258 leading, the pair are waiting for the signal to head the short distance westwards to Cardiff's Canton depot for stabling.

In April 1994, 37797 waits at Newport station for the signal to move off westwards. To the right is the Godfrey Road stabling point, all trace of which has now long gone.

During the same month, it is the turn of Civil Engineer's department-liveried 37230 to pause in Newport station. The loco is working a rake of loaded ballast wagons.

The use of Class 37 locomotives on rakes of merry-go-round (MGR) coal wagons was a regular occurrence through the decade. On 5 April 1990, 37704 heads west through the Valley Lines platforms at Cardiff's Central station.

In October 1991, 37902 *British Steel Llanwern* is seen stabled on Cardiff Canton depot. On that day, the loco is buffered up to the depot's resident breakdown train.

A little later in the day, 37902 is joined by sister loco, 37704, which makes a trio of Class 37 locomotives awaiting their next duties. The Class 37/9 sub-class was created in the mid-1980s incorporating a number of modifications to the six locomotives involved. These six locos, 37901 to 37906, were also to be a testbed for the proposed new Class 38. That project was subsequently shelved.

In this 1994 scene at Newport, an HST waits in platform 2 on a service to London Paddington. At the same time, 37711 heads in the opposite direction through platform 1 on a westbound tank working.

Another coal working is seen heading east through Cardiff Central in April 1994. Loco 37799 *Sir Dyfed County of Dyfed* is providing the power for the MGR coal wagons; the loco appropriately carries the Railfreight Coal Sector decals.

Brush Type '4' locomotives are also regularly found along the SWML, including light-engine movements to and from Godfrey Road stabling point. On 18 April 1994, 47395 and 47309 *The Halewood Transmission* pause on Newport's centre line.

Both locos were built in the mid-1960s and were operated by Railfreight Distribution when seen here at Newport. 47309 was cut up in 2009 at T. J. Thompson in Stockton. Sister loco 47395 has however survived as 47205. It is currently owned by Northampton & Lamport Railway.

A third Class 47 locomotive remained on Newport's Godfrey Road stabling point that afternoon. 47347 is seen there sporting its Railfreight Metals decals.

Brush Type '4', 47188, is seen heading eastbound light engine through Cardiff Central in April 1994. The loco is sporting the Railfreight Distribution's sector decals.

On 12 October 1991, Network South East-liveried 47707 *Holyrood* is a less common visitor to the Cardiff Canton depot. It was particularly surprising to find it here as the author had been hauled by this loco just a few days earlier between London Waterloo and Basingstoke.

The 1990s also saw the use of Class 56 locomotives on MGR coal trains in South Wales. In April 1990, 56030 *Eggborough Power Station* waits to head west from Cardiff Central on one of these coal workings.

Three years later, in 1993, it's the turn of 56073 *Tremorfa Steelworks* to put in an appearance at Cardiff Central. It is slowing for a red signal in the centre road while hauling a westbound coal working.

A visit to Cardiff Canton in April 1994 found another Railfreight Coal Sector loco, 56125, stabled on the depot. It is seen in the company of a Class 37 loco and a Class 08 diesel shunter.

The beginning of the 1990s also saw the commencement of the delivery of the Class 60 loco fleet which were to see a thirty-year association with freight traffic in South Wales. In April 1990, a newly delivered 60004 *Lochnagar* is seen stabled on Cardiff Canton.

A visit to the same depot three weeks later and 60004 is there again. Sporting its new Railfreight Coal Sector decals, it was to be one of forty-two out of the total fleet of 100 to be used by this sector.

With the ever-present breakdown train for company, 60034 *Carnedd Llewelyn* has just arrived on the depot at Canton. An unidentified Class 47 is seen in the background with an eastbound freight train on the SWML completing this April 1994 scene.

In October 1991, 60020 *Great Whernside* heads east through Cardiff Central. It is hauling a Port Talbot to Llanwern working.

In this 1994 view, 60036 *Sgurr Na Ciche* is seen heading in the opposite direction, travelling west with a rake of empties.

A couple of weeks later, sister Class 60 loco 60096 *Ben Macdui* passes through Newport station. It is one of a batch of ten Class 60s which have been in use with GB Railfreight since 2018. A Regional Railways Class 158 is calling in platform 2.

Following the rail privatisation in the mid-1990s the entire fleet of 100 Class 60 locomotives passed into the ownership of DB Cargo (then English, Welsh & Scottish Railway). The company's maroon and gold livery was in the process of being applied to their fleet, including 60022, seen here passing light engine through Newport in 1999.

Freight in South Wales Since Privatisation

In the mid-1990s, rail privatisation was to see a major change to freight operations in South Wales. Space precludes a full account of how this process evolved, but suffice to say that English, Welsh & Scottish Railway (EWS) was to be the main beneficiary in the area. A derelict-looking platform 4 is the backdrop for this 1999 scene at Newport. EWS-liveried 60041 has just arrived light engine. It will shortly reverse back onto Godfrey Road stabling point.

In 1999, the ubiquitous Class 66 locos also made their first appearances in South Wales. These General Motors machines were systematically to replace many of the older locomotives that EWS had inherited in the division of British Rail's assets. This westbound MGR working sees 66073 pass through Newport station a little later the same day.

On 29 April 1999, 66097 was also employed on MGR coal traffic. This time the location is Cardiff Central station as the loco heads west.

Also in April 1999, another light-engine move through Newport sees EWS-liveried 37668 about to reverse onto Godfrey Road stabling point. Remarkably, this loco, built as D6957 back in 1965, has survived and has been in the operational fleet of West Coast Railway since 2014.

In the twenty-first century, EWS was rebranded, first as DB Schenker in 2009 and then as DB Cargo in 2016. Since the downturn in railborne coal traffic, the steel traffic provides DB Cargo with a sizeable percentage of their freight revenue in the area. On 14 July 2015, 60020 heads west through Cardiff Central on a working from East Usk Yard, Newport, to Margam.

A pair of Class 66 locos, 66051 and 66250, head west through Newport station on 30 May 2012. They are working the return empty steel-coil wagons from Corby, in Northamptonshire, to Margam.

On 16 September 2019, 66078 passes through Newport station in the opposite direction. It is taking a rake of loaded steel coils from Margam to Llanwern.

Another longstanding steel flow links the yard at Margam with the West Midlands steel terminal at Round Oak, Brierley Hill. A rake of empty wagons, hauled by 66011, is seen approaching Severn Tunnel Junction on the return working to Margam.

Much of this steel traffic emanates from Tata's giant steelworks at Port Talbot. This is a 2017 view of the yards there, with one of Tata's shunters at work.

The complex is adjacent to Margam Knuckle Yard, from where the rail traffic is despatched to various sites around the UK. Tata shunter 261 *Ed Murray* is about to return from the Knuckle Yard to the steelworks yard.

Margam Knuckle Yard is also the stabling point for DB Cargo's locomotives in the Port Talbot area. On 10 November 2017, their Class 60 locomotive 60040 *The Territorial Army Centenary* is seen stabled in the yard.

In this second photo of 60040, taken later the same week, the variety of wagons stabled at Margam is evident. The view is looking eastwards in the Cardiff direction.

On 6 May 2019, the Margam locomotive stabling point is home to Class 60 60007 *The Spirit of Tom Kendall.* It is flanked by a pair of Class 66 locomotives, 66108 and 66158, with one unidentified sister loco behind.

On 2 July 2021, 66199 is seen approaching Margam Knuckle Yard from the west. The loco is hauling a short rake of SSA scrap wagons from Jersey Marine, near Swansea.

Another rake of SSA wagons is seen being hauled through Cardiff Central on 14 July 2015. DB Schenker's Class 66 66086 heads west with a working from Port Talbot to Aldwarke, in South Yorkshire.

On 30 June 2021, 66129 is seen heading a short rake of empty steel wagons as it passes west through Cardiff Central station. This is one of the regular workings linking Llanwern and Margam. As I write these notes, the future of the Tata steelworks at Port Talbot is uncertain, with inevitable consequences to railborne freight volumes and DB Cargo, in particular.

The next day at Cardiff Central, 1 July 2021, DB Cargo's 66192 is seen passing through the Valley Lines platforms as it works empty coal hoppers from Margam to Cwmbargoed. These workings were to be some of the last seeing coal moved by rail anywhere in the UK. The Ffos-y-Fran open-cast mine had operated since 2007 with trains of loaded coal running from nearby Cwmbargoed to the Margam/Port Talbot complex. The last working was in February 2024. The rail facility at Cwmbargoed is at the end of a freight-only line that runs for about 20 miles from its junction at Ystrad Mynach.

DB Cargo's Class 60 fleet has been considerably reduced in favour of the Class 66s. Their small fleet of surviving Class 60 locomotives have, however, been the motive power of choice to continue to haul the heavy, loaded oil-tank trains along the South Wales Main Line. On 16 September 2019, 60015 heads through Newport on a loaded working from Robeston oil refinery to the oil terminal at Westerleigh, near Bristol.

On 15 July 2014, sister Class 60, 60040 *The Territorial Army Centenary* heads the returning empty tanks through Cardiff Central. The demise of DB Cargo's fleet of Class 60 locomotives has recently seen a change in motive power for these services.

As can be seen from these two photos, the single Class 60 locomotive has now been replaced with a pair of DB Cargo's Class 66 locomotives. On 30 June 2021, 66112 and 66101 are paired as they pass Severn Tunnel Junction station. This is the empty wagon working returning from Westerleigh, Bristol, to Robeston in West Wales.

The loaded working is seen in this view on 7 March 2024. The pairing of 66006 and 66115 pass through Cardiff Central's centre roads as they head for the Westerleigh branch.

The Godfrey Road stabling point at Newport has long gone, and DB Cargo locos in the Newport area stable to the west of the tunnel, at Alexandra Dock Junction. On 16 September 2019, 66125 is seen stabled in the yard there.

On 26 May 2012, 59002 makes a welcome change from the regular Class 66 movements as it heads through Newport station. It is heading to Alexandra Dock Junction stabling point. These Class 59s were, in part, the prototypes for the Class 66 fleet.

Passing freight trains are becoming an increasingly rare event along the South Wales Main Line. In September 2019, two steel trains meet at Cardiff Central. A double-headed working with 66097 and 66017 heading west meets 66144 heading east.

On 21 February 2018, DB Cargo's 60054 waits for the signal to head west on a Llanwern to Margam working. On the adjacent track, Colas Rail's 70812 is also waiting to head west. It is on a working from Avonmouth Docks to Aberthaw Power Station.

Freightliner containers have been a familiar sight on Britain's railways since the mid-1960s. In the mid-1990s, Freightliner became a privately owned rail business following a management buyout. The terminal at Wentloog, on the outskirts of Cardiff, has been an important part of that UK network of container terminals. With convenient access to the M4 motorway, the rail terminal is next to the South Wales Main Line, to the east of Cardiff. In September 2019, Freightliner Class 66 loco 66541 is seen at the terminal's obscured entrance.

Later the same day, the loco is seen passing through Newport station taking its train from Cardiff Wentloog to the Port of Felixstowe. This journey will operate via the Great Western Main Line, the North London line round the capital and then the Great Eastern Main Line to reach the Suffolk port.

On 6 July 2013, 66590 is also seen passing through Newport station. This time the train is heading west on an inbound container service to Cardiff Wentloog.

The Welsh terminal also sees regular container traffic to and from the South Coast of England's Port of Southampton. On 30 June 2021, 66520 approaches the station platforms at Severn Tunnel Junction. This container train is a working from Cardiff Wentloog and is bound for Southampton's Maritime Freight Terminal.

The South Wales Main Line sees a short-distance working linking Wentloog with Barry Docks on the Vale of Glamorgan line. On 17 September 2019, 66553 climbs up to Cardiff Central with a Barry Docks working.

A year earlier, on 22 February 2018, it's the turn of 66529 to pass through Cardiff Central station on a service to Barry Docks. In February 2015, American company Genesee and Wyoming Inc. had acquired a 95 per cent stake in Freightliner.

In the last few years, Freightliner's Heavy Haul Division has suffered considerably from the downturn in coal traffic as a result of closures of all but one of the UK's coal-fired power stations. This has made scenes such as this one something of a rarity in South Wales in recent years. In February 2018, 66522 heads east through Cardiff Central with a rake of hoppers working from Onllwyn Washery to Scunthorpe.

On 16 September 2019, 66602 is seen heading through Newport station with a westbound rake of hoppers. They are working from the yard at Stoke Gifford, in Bristol, to Port Talbot.

In November 2017, Freightliner's 66587 is an interloper in DB Cargo 'territory' at Margam Knuckle Yard. It stands alongside DB Cargo's 66150, which has just arrived in the yard on a mixed rake of empty steel wagons.

Direct Rail Services also operate into the container terminal at Cardiff Wentloog. They have a regular daily working to and from the railfreight terminal at Daventry, Northamptonshire. This service is operated on behalf of Tesco, using their own branded 'Less CO2 Rail' containers. On 13 November 2017, 66433 hauls the westbound working through Severn Tunnel Junction on its way to the Wentloog terminal.

The emergence of GB Railfreight (GBRf) as a major player in the UK rail-freight market has come about since the era of rail privatisation. At the time of writing, they have yet to make substantial inroads into their competitors' Welsh freight traffic, as they have elsewhere in the UK. On 25 May 2012, 66715 *Valour* is seen heading west through Newport station on a rake of wagons containing scrap destined for Cardiff Tidal.

Sister GB Railfreight loco 66753 *EMD Roberts Road* is also seen passing through Newport station. This time the date is 16 July 2015 and the working is eastbound from Pengam to Avonmouth.

On 17 September 2019, 66745 *Modern Railways The First 50 Years* approaches Cardiff Central with another rake of wagons working from Pengam. This time the train is heading in the opposite direction through Cardiff to its destination at Neath.

On 30 June 2021, GBRf's 66752 *The Hoosier State* powers through Cardiff Central with a rake of ferry vans. This working operates from Tilbury, in Essex, to Tata's tinplate works at Trostre, near Llanelli.

Colas Rail's presence in South Wales was highlighted by their 2012 acquisition of the Pullman Rail business based at Cardiff, alongside the Canton rail depot. The company's locos soon became regulars through Cardiff Central station. On 21 May that year, 66850 heads light engine east through the station. This loco was one of five acquired from Freightliner and was numbered 66577 under their ownership. The Pullman business was to be sold to Transport for Wales in 2021.

In November 2017, sister loco 66849 *Wylam Dilly*, formerly Freightliner's 66576, is seen at Cardiff working an empty log-wagon train between Chirk and Baglan Bay, near Swansea. The customer is Kronospan, Colas's first freight client, based at Chirk, between Wrexham and Oswestry.

On this day in July 2014, Colas's choice of locomotive for this working was one of their Class 56s, 56113. The loaded train is seen eastbound through Cardiff's Central station.

The empty log-carrying wagons are seen passing Newport on 6 March 2024, hauled by another of Colas Rail's fleet of Class 56 locomotives, 56051 *Survival*. The logs are taken by road from the Afan Forest area to the sidings at Baglan Bay for loading onto these wagons for the return to Kronospan at Chirk.

The Colas Rail Class 70 locomotives also made regular appearances in South Wales when the power station at Aberthaw was still operational. In February 2018, 70812 approaches Severn Tunnel Junction with a rake of empty hoppers from Aberthaw to Avonmouth Docks. The Aberthaw Power Station closed in March 2020.

The nearby Lafarge Cement Works at Aberthaw is the destination for this Colas Rail working from Westbury. On 16 September 2019, 70808 heads west through Newport. It will reach its destination to the west of Barry via the Vale of Glamorgan line.

Local Passenger Trains in
the Nationalised Era

As mentioned earlier, a limited number of the first generation of diesel multiple units survived into the 1990s on local traffic in South Wales. Metropolitan Cammell three-car unit C388 arrives at Cardiff Central in October 1991. The set is formed of cars 53164, 59387 and 53203.

A year earlier, on 5 April 1990, two-car set C976 has just terminated at Central station. The unit, built in 1960 by BR at Derby Works, was formed of cars 51417 and 54212.

At the beginning of the 1990s, new Class 150 'Sprinter' units were starting to appear on Valley Lines services. In this view, also from April 1990, 150267 is departing Cardiff Central on a service from Caerphilly to Penarth.

Another 'Sprinter' class variant, the two-car Class 155 numbered 155333 is seen at Cardiff Central in 1991 waiting to take up its next duty. Under Regional Railways, these units were soon to be separated into a pair of single-car Class 153 units from each 155 set.

The Iconic High Speed Trains

It is a testimony to the InterCity 125 High Speed Trains that these Class 43 power cars were first introduced in the mid-1970s and some remain in traffic half a century later. This is a typical scene of these iconic machines meeting at Cardiff Central station in their early days.

By the 1990s, the familiar InterCity livery had been applied to these diesel power cars. Car number 43173 has just terminated at Cardiff on a service from London Paddington.

In this 1994 view of Newport, 43005 brings up the rear of this service calling on a London Paddington working. The calling pattern of these London services has remained virtually unchanged in the last thirty years, with all trains making a stop here.

Sister power car 43034 is seen at Newport earlier the same day. It is also bound for London Paddington, this time on a service that had originated at Swansea.

Unlike today, in this mid-1990s view of InterCity power car 43016 *Garden Festival of Wales 1992/Gŵyl Gerddi Cymru 1992* it is the lack of buildings on the skyline that demonstrates how much the Welsh capital has changed in the last thirty years. There is, of course, no electrification in evidence either as the train readies for departure to London Paddington.

The livery on these power cars was to change as privatisation took hold. In this view at Newport on 12 April 2006, power car 43004 is seen sporting the First Great Western livery. It also carried the appropriate nameplates *First for the Future/First ar gyfr y dyfodol*.

These impressive machines are best viewed when passing at speed. In November 2017, a complete set of First Great Western-liveried stock passes Margam Knuckle Yard on a Swansea to London Paddington service. Power car 43153 is leading, with 43163 bringing up the rear.

The Newport skyline has also changed a great deal since this view, as has the appearance of InterCity power car 43172. It is seen calling on a London service in April 1994.

Two decades later, 43172 was chosen to carry a 'celebrity' livery honouring *Harry Patch – the last survivor of the trenches*. The power car is seen arriving at Cardiff Central on 9 November 2017 to form a London Paddington service. It had recessed in the nearby sidings alongside Cardiff Canton.

Even after the use of HSTs on London services had ceased, Great Western Railway continued to use their power cars with shorter coaching stock formations on their West of England services, including Cardiff to Taunton and beyond. These 'Castle' sets were typically formed of four coaches within the twin power cars, as seen here at Cardiff on 30 June 2021. Power car 43154 *Compton Castle* is the power car, nearest the camera, at the rear.

Another 'Castle' set is seen approaching the platform at Severn Tunnel Junction earlier the same day. This time the power car combination is 43094 *St Mawes Castle* leading, with 43170 *Chepstow Castle* on the rear. This latter power car was exported to Mexico in August 2023.

Caring for the Infrastructure

Over the last thirty years a variety of rolling stock has been seen in South Wales in connection with maintenance of the railway infrastructure. On 5 April 1990, a three-car departmental diesel multiple unit approaches Cardiff Central. It is formed of car numbers 977391 plus 999602 plus 977392.

A small fleet of High Speed Train power cars were commandeered by Network Rail to be used to power the New Measurement Train (NMT). Power car 43062 *John Armitt* is seen on the rear of this train as it heads west through Cardiff Central station in November 2017. In common with other stock, these HSTs were to be re-liveried in the familiar Network Rail yellow.

South Wales also sees regular visits from a variety of track machines. On 5 March 2024, Colas Rail's tamper DR73907 is seen stabled at Cardiff Canton.

In autumn each year, a number of Rail Head Treatment Trains (RHTT) operate across the rail network. These trains aim to counter wheel slip when the leaf fall is at its peak and crushed leaves become embedded on the rail tracks. In November 2017, DB Cargo's 66117 and 66047 top 'n' tail one of these trains, seen on the Vale of Glamorgan line at Llantwit Major.

CrossCountry Trains

For most of the privatised era, the longer distance trains linking the South West of England with the North of England and Scotland have been operated by Arriva, under the CrossCountry (XC) branding. These services are centred on Birmingham's New Street station and operated by XC's fleet of Voyager diesel units. On 16 July 2015, 220032 waits to pull forward at Cardiff Central to pick up passengers heading to the north.

On 1 July 2017, sister Voyager 220001 waits to form an early morning service to Bristol. South Wales has gradually seen the removal of these direct longer distance services, although, as I write these notes, a new direct service linking Cardiff and Edinburgh is believed to be under consideration.

The remaining CrossCountry services in South Wales link Cardiff with the Midlands cities of Birmingham, Derby and Nottingham. On 21 June 2014, Class 170 three-car unit 170102 is waiting at Cardiff Central to form a returning service to Nottingham.

A pair of these units are seen passing in Newport station on 16 September 2019. On the right, 170107 waits to head to Cardiff, while 170518 is seen on the left with a Nottingham service. These trains operate via Chepstow and Gloucester to reach Cheltenham and Birmingham.

Great Western Railway Services to England's South Coast and South West

For most of the privatised era, Great Western Railway (GWR) has also operated services across the English border to destinations including Portsmouth Harbour, Taunton and Penzance. A variety of motive power has been used on these services, including 150104, seen leaving Newport in July 2013 on a Cardiff to Taunton service. The unit carries the First Great Western branding.

Four years later, a similar service calls at Severn Tunnel Junction on 13 November 2017 operated by three-car Class 150 unit 150002. The company branding was in the process of being changed to Great Western Railway, including the application of a base green livery reflecting the days of the Great Western Railway. This distinctive livery was in use from the 1830s through to the formation of British Railways at the end of 1947.

GWR also operate an hourly service linking Cardiff with Portsmouth Harbour, via Bristol, Westbury, Salisbury and Southampton. The company's Class 158 units were the mainstay on these services for many years. Three-car unit 158952 waits at Cardiff to form a Portsmouth Harbour service on 21 June 2014.

Sister unit 158798 is seen on a service heading in the opposite direction in November 2017 as it passes through Severn Tunnel Junction heading for Cardiff. This unit carries a one-off livery promoting the charity Springboard.

Class 165 and Class 166 'Turbo' diesel units, displaced from further east, have since commenced use on GWR services to and from Cardiff. In September 2019, 165118 leads a five-car rake waiting to pull forward to form an eastbound service.

On 7 March 2024, 166211 waits in the same position in platform 2. It will shortly pull forward to form the 07.28 service to Portsmouth Harbour. The end-to-end journey of just over 100 miles takes around 3½ hours.

A number of services between Cardiff and Bristol and the West of England have recently seen a switch to IET haulage. On 6 March 2024, 802020 arrives at Newport working a slightly delayed service from Bristol Temple Meads to Cardiff Central.

The previous day, 800026 is seen terminating at Cardiff Central on an early morning arrival from the West of England.

South Wales Main Line (SWML) Electrification

The SWML was one of the last major InterCity routes in the UK to be electrified. The electric power westward from London was switched on in stages and finally through to Cardiff at the end of 2019. This 2015 view shows the electrification work in progress at Severn Tunnel Junction. Initially, Great Western Railway were to be the main beneficiaries, with electrification of their services to London Paddington.

The Intercity Express Programme (IEP) was developed by Hitachi to provide a fleet of replacements for the High Speed Trains, including between London Paddington and South Wales. To facilitate the servicing of this rolling stock, a new depot was constructed at Swansea Maliphant. This is the view of the construction in November 2017.

Hitachi developed a series of Intercity Express Trains (IETs) for Great Western Railway (GWR) to use on these services, including a fleet of bi-mode units. This included a fleet of thirty-six Class 800/0 five-car units. One of these, 800013, is seen passing though Severn Tunnel Junction on a Swansea to London service.

In this September 2019 view, five-car unit 800032 leaves Newport on a Cardiff to London Paddington service. At this time, it continued to operate in diesel mode as the overhead electric current was yet to go live.

GWR provides a half-hourly IET service between London and Cardiff throughout the day, with one train an hour continuing westwards to Swansea and, sometimes, Carmarthen. On 17 September 2019, nine-car variant 800316 approaches Cardiff Central on a terminating service from London Paddington.

The on-off saga of electrification west of Cardiff would appear to be off for the longer term. This leaves services between Carmarthen and Swansea to London operating on diesel power to the west of Cardiff. On 10 November 2017, 800008 and 800009 pass Margam on a westbound service.

Loco-hauled Passenger Trains to Manchester and Holyhead

Since privatisation, most services within South Wales have been in the hands of Arriva Trains Wales and, more recently, Transport for Wales. DB Cargo Class 67 diesel locomotives have been used on a number of these services between South Wales and both Holyhead and Manchester Piccadilly. On 15 July 2014, 67003 approaches Newport on a service to Holyhead. At the time, the loco was outshopped in the dedicated turquoise livery of Arriva Trains Wales.

These locomotives are maintained by DB Cargo staff outbased at Cardiff Canton depot. On 5 March 2024, 67007 is stabled on the depot awaiting its next duty. This locomotive carries the distinctive Platinum Jubilee livery. These Class 67 locomotives operate with a Driving Vehicle Trailer (DVT) at the opposite end of the train.

Sister loco 67010 is seen arriving at Cardiff Central on 1 July 2021. The train is terminating at the end of a circuitous 230-mile journey from Holyhead that has taken around 4½ hours with a 10.00 arrival in Cardiff following a 05.30 departure from Holyhead.

This Class 67 locomotive haulage arrangement has continued under the auspices of Transport for Wales. Their livery has been applied to 67025, seen here awaiting departure from Cardiff Central on 7 March 2024. The train is the 08.49 departure to Manchester Piccadilly; it will take just under 3½ hours to complete the 170-mile journey.

Loco-hauled Passenger Trains in the Valleys

Locomotive-hauled passenger trains made a temporary return to the Rhymney line in 2019, with some services operated by hired-in Class 37 diesel locomotives. On 17 September 2019, Colas Rail's 37421 trundles down the incline from Cardiff Queen Street on a morning commuter service from Rhymney.

Another Class 37 celebrity, 37025 *Inverness TMD Quality Approved*, is seen stabled on Cardiff Canton sidings in September 2019. It has just arrived on the empty coaching stock from Cardiff Central, having delivered its Rhymney line passengers there. This particular locomotive is owned by the Scottish 37 Group.

Class 142 and Class 143 'Pacers', 1985–2020

A total of ninety-four Class 142 'Pacer' units were built for the nationalised rail network in the mid-1980s. In the privatised era, Arriva Trains Wales were to put their allocation of these units to work, chiefly on the local Valley and Vale of Glamorgan lines. On 5 June 2019, 142002 arrives at Ninian Park on a City Line service to Coryton.

These units were to knock up several million miles in service before their final withdrawal in 2020. They were often worked in pairs to cater for extra customer demand but did not benefit from a 'walk-through' facility between units when so doing. On 8 November 2017, 142077 and 142006 are paired as they leave Caerphilly on a Rhymney line service towards Penarth.

These 'Pacers' were also to be found on services between Maesteg and Cheltenham Spa. On 13 November 2017, 142010 calls at Severn Tunnel Junction on a Cheltenham-bound working.

As will be seen later in this publication, electrification mast installation is well advanced on the Treherbert line, with the last but one station on the branch, Ynyswen, temporarily closed in connection with this work. Back in 2017, 142083 makes a call at the single-platform station on its way to Treherbert.

A small fleet of Class 143 'Pacer' variants has been based at Cardiff Canton since the early 1990s. They were regularly employed on Valley Lines services, including the Rhymney line. In November 2017, 143624 terminates at Ystrad Mynach on one such service.

The following day in November 2017, sister unit 143609 is seen calling at Tonypandy. It is working a Treherbert to Cardiff Central service.

Passenger services were originally withdrawn on the Ebbw Vale line in the 1960s. Services were reinstated to Ebbw Vale Parkway in 2008, and a few years later in 2015 a further extension was opened to Ebbw Vale Town. In November 2017, 143602 waits at Town station to return to Cardiff. In early 2024, direct passenger services were also introduced between Ebbw Vale Town and Newport.

To say that the 'Pacers' were an unpopular passenger train would be a huge understatement. Their impending demise in 2020 brought about an unprecedented re-branding by TfW, reassuring passengers that 'These trains will terminate soon'. This is unit 143606 so branded, seen in June 2019.

Class 150, 153 and 158 Units Soldier On

A fleet of Class 150 'Sprinter' units was manufactured by British Rail Engineering Ltd in the late 1980s. They operated numerous regional services across the UK, including a fleet based in Wales. Currently, thirty-four of these two-car units are based at Cardiff Canton, operated by TfW. In November 2017, 150255 stands at the terminus at Swansea waiting to work a Heart of Wales Line service to Shrewsbury.

These units require reversal at Llanelli prior to heading north-westwards to Shrewsbury. On 12 November 2017, it's the turn of unit 150240 to reverse at Llanelli station, while working the 11.32 service to Shrewsbury.

These popular workhorses have worked across most of Wales for almost forty years, including to terminus stations to the west of Swansea. On 11 November 2017, 150285 waits at the forlorn-looking single-platform station at Pembroke Dock. It will shortly depart forming the 15.09 return service to Swansea.

These Class 150 units continue to see use on the Valley Lines services, including the Merthyr line to and from Aberdare. A passing loop constructed at Mountain Ash in 2002 enabled a half-hourly service to operate. In November 2017, a pair of these units, 150282 and 150250, meet in Mountain Ash station's passing loop.

Since the 1990s, a fleet of single-car Class 153 units have been based in Wales. These were converted from the former two-car Class 155 units, an example of which is seen on p. 50. On 21 November 2013, 153362 calls at Newport on a service to Cheltenham Spa.

For much of the last thirty years, these Class 153 units have worked services between Swansea and Shrewsbury on the Heart of Wales Line, with some journeys extended from Swansea to Cardiff. In June 2019, 153320 heads towards Cardiff on one such service. It is approaching Margam Knuckle Yard.

On 4 June 2019, a pair of Class 153 units, 153312 and 153362, are seen approaching Cardiff Central on a Valley Lines service. Coincidentally, these two were permanently coupled together as unit 155312 until being split in 1992.

In the 2020s, Transport for Wales became the only operator to continue the use of these single-car units, having carried out the necessary modifications to comply with the Persons with Reduced Mobility Specifications. Sporting Transport for Wales livery, 153913 is seen waiting departure from Cardiff Central on 7 March 2024, working 07.51 City Line service to Coryton. A few modified examples remain in use with Scotrail, but only to strengthen existing Class 156 formations.

Almost 200 Class 158 units were delivered by British Rail Engineering Ltd in the late 1980s and early 1990s during the nationalised era of Regional Railways. On 13 November 2017, 158828 is seen at Severn Tunnel Junction on a Cheltenham Spa to Maesteg service.

Since 2007, the twenty-four units operating in Wales have been primarily based at Machynlleth in Central Wales. They do, however, still see service along the South Wales Main Line, with TfW-liveried 158822 seen here at Newport on 16 September 2019.

Class 170 and Class 769 Units – Short-term Use in South Wales

A small fleet of Class 170 units was based at Cardiff's Canton depot in the early 2020s, including three-car unit 170202, seen here calling at Severn Tunnel Junction on 30 June 2021. These units were used on the Cheltenham Spa to Maesteg service between 2020 and 2023.

Sister three-car unit 170201 is seen at Cardiff Central station the following day, ready to head for Cheltenham Spa. This batch of twelve units was transferred in from Greater Anglia and, very quickly, transferred away again, this time to East Midlands Railway.

The changing skyline at Cardiff is evident above 170207 in this 2021 view. These units were also used on services linking Cardiff with Ebbw Vale Town. They ranked particularly highly in local customer service feedback.

Another short-lived plan saw a total of nine bi-mode Class 769 'Flex' units operate local services from Cardiff's Canton depot. These units were conversions from former Network SouthEast Class 319 units, ordered in the nationalised era of the late 1980s. Unit 769006 is seen approaching Cardiff Central in June 2021. These units were introduced in South Wales in 2020 and withdrawn three years later.

Class 175 Units, 1997–2023

Initially ordered for the First North Western franchise, the Class 175 diesel multiple units were to spend most of their working lives on services for the Arriva Trains Wales franchise. A fleet of twenty-seven units had been commissioned from Alstom in 1997, with delivery around the turn of the millennium. On 2 June 2012, the first-numbered unit, 175001, awaits its next duty at Cardiff Central.

Several members of the class can be seen in this view of Carmarthen early on a Sunday morning. On 12 November 2017, 175009 is to the left of the photo while 175002 prepares to depart on an eastbound service.

The previous day, three-car variant 175105 waits at Whitland as passengers join the 09.46 service from there to Manchester Piccadilly. These units proved particularly unpopular with a number of issues requiring action during their two decades of operation.

By the time this photo was taken in November 2019 the revised TfW livery had started to be applied to these units, including 175002, seen here at Newport. By February 2023, this unit had been placed in store, with return to lessor Angel Trains a few months later. The entire fleet was to be withdrawn by the end of that year.

New Order for the 2020s – Class 197 Units

In 2018, Keolis/Amey ordered a fleet of new diesel units as part of its franchise obligations to Transport for Wales. These diesel multiple units were split between fifty-one two-car units and twenty-six three-car units, to be designated as Class 197s. They were based on the Class 195s already on delivery in Northern England. These Class 197 trains were built by Spanish Manufacturer Construcciones y Auxiliar de Ferrocarriles (CAF), with the first unit being commissioned in the UK in 2021. On 6 March 2024, three-car unit 197106 approaches Newport on a Maesteg to Cheltenham Spa service.

These CAF units were assembled at a purpose-built company facility at Newport and were specifically built by the company to provide new trains within the UK market. As if to proudly mark this commitment to the Welsh labour market, unit 197120 is seen at Cardiff Central including 'Made in Wales' vinyls.

These units were built after customer feedback had been received elsewhere in the UK. As a result, the seats, described by many users of similar CAF classes as 'ironing boards', were enhanced. Additionally, the Class 197s have an increased number of toilet facilities. As deliveries continue, their use is becoming more widespread across Wales. On 6 March 2024, 197104 passes Margam Knuckle Yard crossing on a service from Carmarthen to Cardiff Central.

The ongoing deliveries of Class 197 units have enabled the less than popular fleet of Class 175 units to be stood down, with the new units replacing them on a variety of diagrams. The smaller fleet of Class 170 units has also been transferred away. In March 2024, another three-car unit, 197109, stops at Pyle on a late-running service to Carmarthen.

These units are also to be found on services linking Manchester Piccadilly with stations in South and West Wales. Two-car unit 197011 is seen arriving at Cardiff's Central station on one such West Wales-bound service in March 2024.

New Order for the 2020s – Class 231 Units

The first class of Fast Light InterCity and Regional Train (FLIRT) units to be built for Transport for Wales by Stadler Rail was an order for eleven four-car diesel units. This order formed part of the Keolis/Amey commitment to replace all rolling stock during the course of their franchise term. These Class 231 units entered service in early 2023. On 5 March 2024, 231004 arrives at Cardiff Central on a service from Penarth to Bargoed.

Later the same day, sister unit 231004 is heading in the opposite direction. It is seen calling at Grangetown on a mid-afternoon service to Penarth. These units are now linking Rhymney, Bargoed and Ystrad Mynach with the capital.

This is an interior view of unit 231005. Given the customers' decades of experience of the Class 142 and Class 143 'Pacers', it is perhaps not surprising that these new, four-car units have been well received by local rail users.

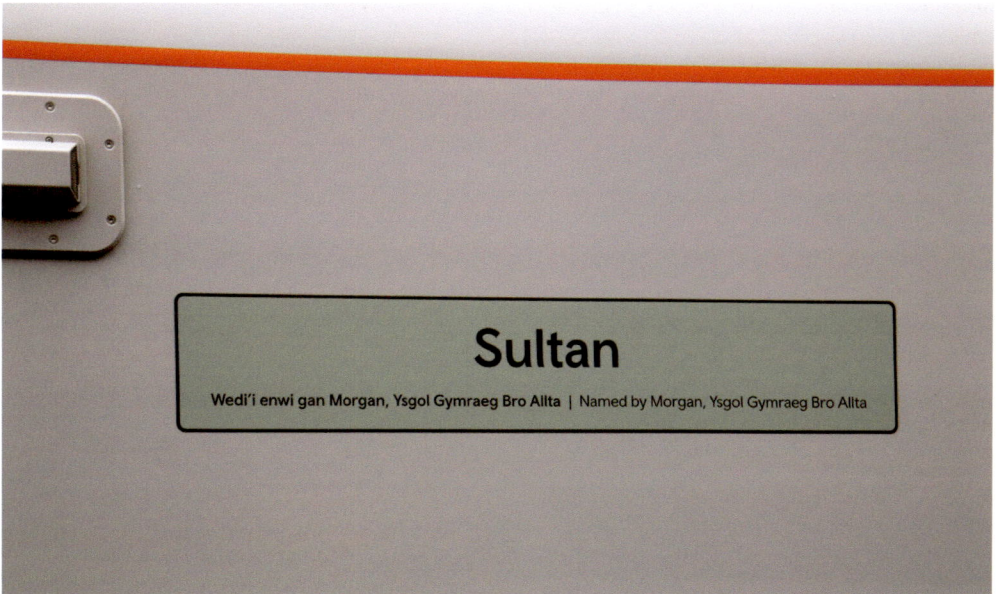

The first Class 231 unit numerically, 231001, was named *Sultan* in March 2023. The name, suggested by local schoolchildren, is taken from that of a Caerphilly statue of a pit pony, acknowledging the non-human work carried out in local collieries. The current diagrams require nine out of eleven of these units in traffic daily.

New Order for the 2020s – Class 398 Units and Electrification in the Valleys

As we've seen, the Class 150 and Class 153 diesel multiple units have provided sterling service across South Wales since the late 1980s and early 1990s. Nevertheless, the Keolis/Amey commitment was to replace all existing rolling stock during the term of the current franchise. This will shortly lead to their withdrawal from service. Their successors are to be a fleet of South Wales Metro Class 398 tram trains based at a new depot at Taffs Well. The new depot is seen here in March 2024.

The Class 398 unit fleet will consist of thirty-six three-car bi-mode tram trains. These are designed to operate on the newly electrified Valley Lines and utilise battery power when operating as a tram on the streets of Cardiff. In this second view of the new Taffs Well depot on the same day, units 398006, 398008, 398014, 398013 and 398010 are stabled from left to right.

The units have been built by Swiss company Stadler Rail at their plant in Valencia, Spain. A total of fifteen units had been delivered by March 2024, including 398005, seen here in the depot area. The depot complex is located approximately 6 miles to the north-west of Cardiff Central station.

A connecting curve into the depot complex from the existing running lines has just been completed. The tightness of this curve can be seen to the left of this view from Taffs Well station footbridge, looking towards Radyr. One of the units to be displaced, 150254, is seen passing on a Bridgend to Aberdare service.

Considerable infrastructure work needs to be completed before these units can enter traffic on services between Cardiff and Treherbert, Aberdare and Merthyr Tydfil. On 6 March 2024, the electrification progress can be seen at the Rhondda-line terminus at Treherbert as 150258 leaves on a service to Cardiff Central.

Although the electrification was initially announced over a decade ago, in 2012, there are still gaps evident in this electrification, as seen here at Treforest. In this March 2024 view, 150237 and 150227 meet on diesel-hauled services. It is unlikely that their electric replacements will enter service before 2025 at the earliest.

The Class 398 units will operate through to Cardiff Bay via new platforms at Central station, including a new station at Butetown. This will effectively see tram trains replace existing trains as part of the wider Cardiff Crossrail project under the control of South Wales Metro. At Cardiff Bay station the work to add a second platform is underway, as seen here in this March 2024 view.

In the meantime, single-car unit 153914 is seen at the existing Cardiff Bay platform on the regular shuttle service to Queen Street. This service will ultimately be replaced by the Class 398 tram trains.

New Order for the 2020s – Class 756 Units

As part of Keolis/Amey's franchise commitment, they undertook to replace the entire TfW fleet during the franchise term. They placed an order for a fleet of Class 756 tri-mode units in February 2019. These were to be based at a new depot built on railway land adjacent to Barry station. This is the view from that station's footbridge in March 2024, with unit 756114 visible in the centre.

This order was for a total of twenty-four Class 756 units, made up of seven three-car units and seventeen four-car units. These closely resemble the Class 755 units previously delivered to Greater Anglia. These Class 756 'FLIRT' units have also been built by Swiss company Stadler Rail. Several of these units can be seen in this second view from Barry station with the line towards Barry Docks running to the left.

Another March 2024 view shows unit 756005 out of use at Barry depot. No start date has been formally announced for their entry in service. Meantime, they are being kept 'warm' with rotational visits to Cardiff Canton depot for routine servicing. They are expected to be used on Rhymney and Vale of Glamorgan line services.

These tri-mode units will operate on electrified lines as well as having a 'power pack' towards the centre of the train that contains both a diesel generator and battery modules. This photo shows a close-up of this power pack on unit 756005.

Other Railway Titles
by the Author